Caught on Camera

Terry Allsop was born in London in 1940 but moved to Grimsby in 1944 because of bomb damage to the family home. Moving back to the Thames Valley in the 1960s, Terry worked for several architectural practices and it was whilst he was employed at the Reading office of Broadway & Malyan that he took most of the photographs in this book.

Also published by Two Rivers Press:

Plant Portraits by Post by Julia Trickey
Allen W. Seaby: Art and nature by Martin Andrews & Robert Gillmor
Reading Detectives by Kerry Renshaw
Fox Talbot & the Reading Establishment by Martin Andrews
Cover Birds by Robert Gillmor
All Change at Reading: The Railway and the Station 1840–2013 by Adam Sowan
An Artist's Year in the Harris Garden by Jenny Halstead
Caversham Court Gardens: A Heritage Guide by Friends of Caversham Court Gardens
Believing in Reading: Our Places of Worship by Adam Sowan
Newtown: A Photographic Journey in Reading 1974 by Terry Allsop
Bikes, Balls & Biscuitmen: Our Sporting Life by Tim Crooks & Reading Museum
Birds, Blocks & Stamps: Post & Go Birds of Britain by Robert Gillmor
The Reading Quiz Book by Adam Sowan
Bizarre Berkshire: An A–Z Guide by Duncan Mackay
Broad Street Chapel & the Origins of Dissent in Reading by Geoff Sawers
Reading Poetry: An Anthology edited by Peter Robinson
Reading: A Horse-Racing Town by Nigel Sutcliffe
Eat Wild by Duncan MacKay
Down by the River: The Thames and Kennet in Reading by Gillian Clark
A Much-maligned Town: Opinions of Reading 1126–2008 by Adam Sowan
A Mark of Affection: The Soane Obelisk in Reading by Adam Sowan
The Stranger in Reading edited by Adam Sowan
The Holy Brook by Adam Sowan
Charms against Jackals edited by Adam Stout and Geoff Sawers
Abattoirs Road to Zinzan Street by Adam Sowan

Caught on Camera
Reading in the 70s

Terry Allsop

TWO
RIVERS
PRESS

First published in the UK in 2015 by Two Rivers Press
7 Denmark Road, Reading RG1 5PA.
www.tworiverspress.com

ISBN 978-1-909747-10-4

1 2 3 4 5 6 7 8 9

Two Rivers Press is represented in the UK by Inpress Ltd and distributed
by Central Books.

Cover photograph Terry Allsop, design by Nadja Guggi.
Text design by Nadja Guggi and typeset in Parisine.

Printed and bound in Great Britain by Ashford Colour Press, Gosport.

Dedications

I dedicate this book to my brother John
who lost his fight against cancer on 11 November 2003.

It was John who gave me the Exacta VX 1000 camera with which
I took the photographs in this book. I hope it is a fitting tribute.

Sadly, it must also be dedicated to two other people,
both of whom have enriched our lives.

For Brenda, our friend for over 40 years, lost her fight
against the same dreadful disease.
She was taken from us on 11 May 2012
to join the angels in heaven.

To Brian, one of the partners of Broadway & Malyan
who is mentioned, although not by name, in the Newtown book.
He sadly passed away on 12 February 2015.

There are no words adequate to express our grief and loss.
They were all very special people.

Acknowledgements

First of all, I must mention my wife Nicola, to recognise all the help and support she has given to me and especially for her secretarial skills in the production of this book. We met when we both worked for Broadway & Malyan, the architects responsible for the many projects, sites and buildings which are featured in this book. What I must record is that her patience is beyond doubt, as we continued to work together at Broadway & Malyan until I retired in 2005. Nicola retired from the practice after completing 36 years of dedicated service with them.

Secondly, I must acknowledge the person who has really made this book, and my previous one, become realities. David Cliffe has contributed so much to bring about the publication of my books. His help, advice and knowledge of the buildings and history of Reading are unparalleled. The exhibitions in Reading Central Library 2009, 2011 and 2014 were the catalysts to get the books published.

Finally and with an extreme sense of gratitude, I must thank Two Rivers Press for having the confidence to take on the task of publishing this book. To Sally, Barbara, Adam and especially to Nadja for producing the graphic design for what is, I think, a most interesting and informative book. And thanks to Anna for coming up with the title!

Contents

Introduction

I took the photographs in this book between the early 1970s and mid 1980s. My previous book, *Newtown: A Photographic Journey in Reading 1974,* recorded a relatively small area in East Reading before many of its buildings were demolished and redeveloped. This book covers a much wider area, incorporating the town centre but also moving beyond to lesser-known places. Many books of urban photographs concentrate on the main shopping streets and well-known landmarks but I have deliberately included back streets and quiet corners. Fortuitously, I was able to capture the face of the town at a time of great change as, during the 40 years since the photographs were taken, major employers like Huntley and Palmers, Suttons Seeds and Courage brewery have given way to technology companies in this, the capital of England's Silicon Valley.

The photographs show people, both young and old, at work, at play and going about their everyday lives, unconcerned about having their photographs taken. It was an age when one could take photographs without being viewed with suspicion. An age of innocence now sadly lost, which is somewhat ironic in this era of camera-phones and 'selfies'. I was able to take photographs of children at work and play in Oxford Road Primary School and pictures from highly unsafe vantage points, such as rooftops and gasometers.

My intention is to try to show how Reading changed during that period, and continues to do so. The majority of the photographs are of buildings that were demolished to make way for redevelopment to take place. Other buildings, whilst they may be standing, have been substantially refurbished, facades have been extended or altered, uses have changed. I hope the photographs featured will help the reader recapture memories of what used to be where.

I have tried to group the photographs geographically but the areas described in each section do sometimes overlap. The reader may wish to take a walk, tracing a route through each section to discover the changes that have taken place. I did consider including photographs taken more recently, to show the buildings that have replaced the ones I recorded all those years ago, but decided against it. A feature of today's Reading is the movement of people back into the central area of the town, with large numbers of residential developments and refurbishment schemes completed, underway and planned for the future.

Some of the major changes that occurred during the period documented in this book are:

- The construction of the Inner Distribution Road (Phase 1) which opened in 1969.

- The closure of Huntley and Palmers which ceased production in 1976.

- Heron House, the Department of Health and Social Services Office Building on Queen's Road, which opened in 1982. It has now been converted into flats.

Later developments, which were started after the period covered by the book, have transformed locations photographed here before work commenced. See if you can recognise the original sites.

- The Oracle Shopping Centre, which opened in 1999.

- Chatham Street Car Park, demolished in 2004, is being replaced with a residential tower block now under construction.

- Kennet House has undergone a change of use and been refurbished to provide residential apartments.

- The Foster Wheeler building is being completely refurbished alongside the extensive demolition and rebuilding of Station Approach.

The last section of the book covers a wide and less geographically-defined area. A number of the photographs feature people going about their everyday lives. This section also contains some mystery photographs. I cannot recall exactly where or when they were taken.

Finally, for those interested in technical details, the camera I used to take the photographs in the 1970s was an Exacta VX1000. It was, I believe, unique in having the shutter release and wind-on mechanism on the left-hand side of the camera.

The station, Station Road, Chatham Street and Caversham Road

In 1840 Brunel gave Reading an inconvenient station with a single platform for trains going in both directions, and separate buildings for London- and Bristol-bound passengers. These were replaced by a single block in 1867, but not until 1900 did the Great Western build more platforms. Very little changed until 1965, when the adjacent Southern station was closed. 1989 brought a footbridge and a new concourse with shops and cafes. The Queen opened this extension and she returned in 2014 to inaugurate the massive 'transfer deck' with lifts and escalators serving yet more platforms. Across the road, the historic Great Western Hotel looks little changed on the outside, but it has undergone considerable alteration within. With a brief detour towards Friar Street, we proceed westwards to Chatham Street and Caversham Road, passing one live pub and two dead ones.

Reading station from the roof of the Great Western Hotel. The 1867
building in the middle, now the Three Guineas pub, was the booking
office. A Reading Corporation bus pulls away as two Railair coaches
wait. Cars are parked freely in front of the station. At bottom right
is a petrol pump in front of Gowrings Motors.

The station from the roof of Foster Wheeler House, now Thames Tower, which at the time of writing is being refurbished and re-clad. A 'tadpole' train from Tonbridge stands at platform 4B. Beyond platform 9 is one of several manual signal boxes that controlled train movements; a signalling centre at Didcot now runs the show. For a full history of the station, see *All Change at Reading* by Adam Sowan.

The dilapidated former Great Western Hotel. One of the earliest railway-connected hotels, it opened in 1844 and closed in about 1972; despite the name it was an independent venture and never run by the railway company.

It was for some time used by the Royal Mail as a sorting office, then in the late 1970s became offices for The Berkshire Area Health Authority, then a solicitor's office. Later it was refurbished and extended, reopening in 2007 as the Malmaison Reading.

The passageway running from Station Road to Friar Street, passing the Garrard Street multi-storey car park. This useful link served the now defunct Friar's Walk shopping mall. The block fronting Station Approach is soon to be redeveloped, having been the subject of discussion for many years.

Butler's Wine Vaults, now The Butler pub on Chatham Street. At this time it still had a separate bar for ladies; the word is etched into the glass in the door. The bottling plant building is on the left. Chatham Street Car Park, in the background, has been replaced by a more attractive version as part of the Chatham Place residential complex.

Another view, showing the rails for the trucks carrying barrels into the bottling plant and off licence in the cobbled area in front of the wall. This part of the pub has now been demolished.

Caversham Road from Abattoirs Road, next to the railway bridge.
The White Horse and Star of India have made way for offices.

Looking in the opposite direction, Caversham Road from Tudor Road. The Duke of Edinburgh appears in an engraving dated 1843, without a signboard; it may have been built by the Great Western as a pair of semi-detached houses for senior staff. This has also been demolished for the Malcolm Place residential apartments.

King's Road and the Kennet

King's Road might now be called Reading's Central Business District. In the 1830s it was an early example of ribbon development, with prosperous houses lining a new main road towards London. These gradually gave way to shops and industrial buildings; then, from the 1960s, a series of large office blocks, some of which are now being converted to flats: perhaps the wheel is coming full circle. Among all this redevelopment, some historic and characterful buildings remain, some of them connected with the Kennet, made navigable to Newbury in 1723 and extended via the Kennet and Avon Canal towards Bristol in 1812. This facilitated the import of Bath stone, which was briefly fashionable in Reading and can be seen further along King's Road. Whatever one thinks of the Oracle, it has at least opened up the waterside through the heart of the town.

The unofficially named Jackson's Corner and the department store which closed in 2014. Many will remember the pneumatic tube system which conveyed payments from the shop counter to the cashier in the basement and brought back the change and receipt. This was one of the last such systems in operation in the country.

Looking back to King Street with J & C Simonds' Bank, owned by the Reading brewing family, built in 1836 and listed Grade II. It was taken over by Barclays in 1913 and closed in 2008. At the time of writing it is awaiting new occupants.

King's Road, opposite Jackson's. Perring's the furnishers occupied
the premises both before and after the site was redeveloped for
Prudential Assurance in the late 1970s. Subsequently it was taken
over by Blackwell's Bookshop: the ground floor now has an estate
agent and a hairdresser, and the upper storeys are flats. They are
labelled 'Il-Libro', preserving a link to bookselling. A sign on a gable
makes one wonder when the last harness was made in this building.

Highbridge Wharf, off King's Road. This listed building, probably built soon after the Kennet and Avon canal opened, has now been beautifully restored, with ground floor windows replacing the garage doors.

On the right, the side of Highbridge Wharf. All the buildings on the left have gone. The canal is behind the photographer.

The canal towpath, looking west to Duke Street and the 1788 High Bridge. The handsome waterside pub in the background, built a century later and known at various times as the Lower Ship or the Horse and Barge, has been boarded up for decades. The buildings in the foreground were all demolished for the Prudential and the associated residential redevelopment in the 1970s.

On the other bank of the canal the former police station and coroner's court, built in 1862 in a curious hispano-gothic style, is now occupied by a firm of solicitors.

A good example of a picture showing the extent of change in the town centre; the Oracle shopping centre now straddles the Kennet. This section of the river was known as the Brewery Gut because the channel flowing through H & G Simonds' premises was narrow, tortuous and fast-flowing, making navigation difficult.

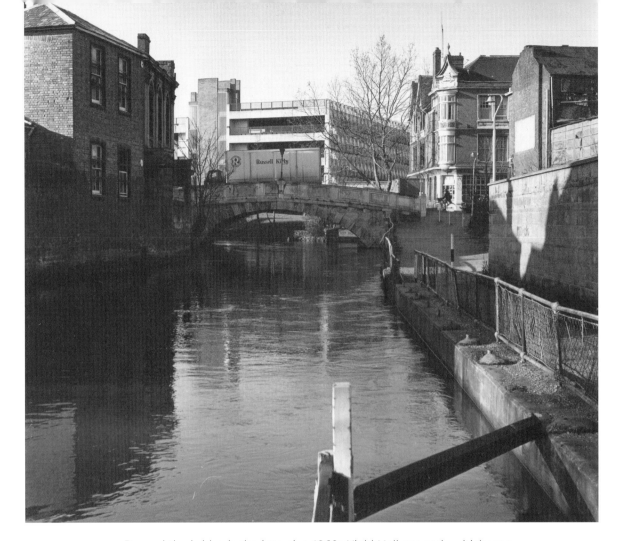

Beyond the bridge is the intrusive 1960s Yield Hall car park, which was approached over a temporary-looking bridge. Debenhams, in the Oracle, now occupies the site.

The High Bridge was originally the Hythe Bridge, meaning a bridge next to a wharf. All the buildings in the background have now been demolished.

The High Bridge from the recessed entrance area to The Lower Ship.

The High Bridge with a man looking at something interesting in the river. The old coroner's court is disused and boarded up.

A place to stop and ponder – or to watch a boat negotiating the tight bend under the low 'high' bridge.

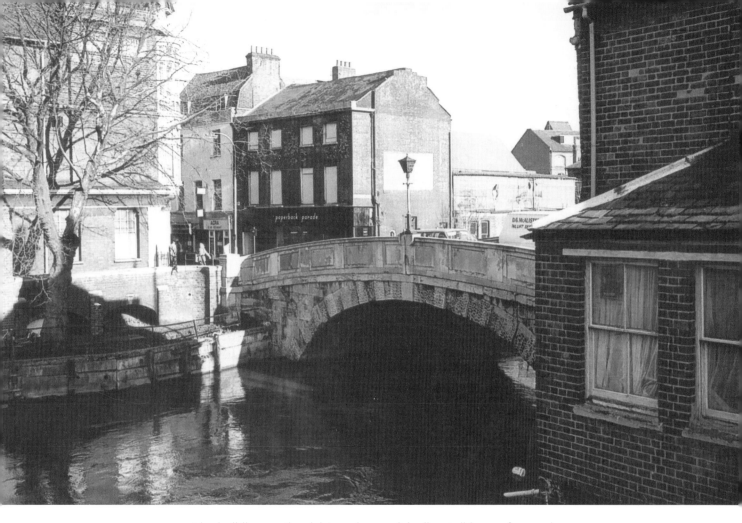

The building on the right, perhaps originally a toll-house for canal traffic, is now the London Street Brasserie. The Lower Ship can be seen behind the tree on the left.

From the top of Yield Hall car park, with the metal access bridge and toll-house.

Thorn Lane, a rare cobbled survivor, from the car park. In the background the 1960s Prudential building was replaced by Forbury Square. Cranes indicate ongoing redevelopment.

The rear of the Ship Hotel (now the Royal County) and the Lower Ship. The parking lot is still there, with the original arched access through the pub to Duke Street on the right, now no longer usable.

The rear of The Ship. The cobbled surface of Thorn Lane is very prominent.

Thorn Lane from the top of the car park, showing the access into the rear of the Lower Ship.

The car park from Yield Hall Place, showing the access tower. The diamond-shaped concrete formers are typical, having also been used for the Chatham Street car park; both have gone.

King's Road with Abbey Square on the left. Reading Central Library
now occupies the site in the central foreground.

Taken from Abbey Square before work on the library started.
Behind the low parapet the Holy Brook flows under the site.

King's Road. The interesting five-storey office building to let was the former Cocks's Reading Sauce Factory. Its replacement was built in a style reminiscent of the original building.

King's Road Baptist church, built in 1834, is for sale in poor condition, with buddleia invading the roof. It was replaced by a modern church in Abbey Square.

The south side of King's Road from near Crown Bridge. Razzmatazz occupies one of the earliest houses, built soon after the road was driven through in 1832. This has now been demolished, but the buildings to the right of it fortunately still remain.

King's Road from near Highbridge Wharf. Most of these buildings have been demolished.

Still in King's Road, this had been a fine late Georgian or early
Victorian terrace; the all-header brick bond with silver-greys
indicates affluence. Sadly, this terrace has also gone.

King's Road with the entrance to Crane Wharf on the left. The four-storey building with gabled windows just to the left of the crane is still there, which cannot be said for all the buildings between it and Crane Wharf, which have become an office block.

Blake's Cottages, across the canal from the prison. Some of the houses at the east end were knocked down when the bridge was widened, and new ones built to the west. The two ladies seem unconcerned about having their photograph taken; the dog is much more interested.

The garden opposite Huntley and Palmers' offices was originally used by the staff; the firm later gave it to the town.

By the canal near Watlington Street bridge, with the Wesley church in the background. A man sits on a planter below Alpha House (now King's Point), an office block which won a Civic Trust Award in 1969. Hoardings with political graffiti surround the residential development next to the Government offices in Queen's Road. At the time of writing, King's Point is showing its age.

Vastern Road, Caversham, the Thames and Newtown

This section covers a larger and more diverse area. Starting in Vastern Road, we briefly cross the Thames, then follow a remarkably quiet route via Caversham Lock to the Clappers. Back in King's Road we meet the Kennet again and touch the fringes of Newtown. (For a comprehensive record of this inner suburb, see my book *Newtown: A Photographic Journey in Reading 1974*).

Vastern Road with Thames Water's Nugent House HQ, now replaced by the circular Clearwater Court. The buildings in the foreground give some idea of the extent of redevelopment which has taken place.

Reading Bridge, looking south to the station.

Christchurch Meadows, with Nugent House and Western Tower in
the background.

Caversham Lock. The lock-keeper's house is no longer occupied.

The lock weir. The walkway could be described as Reading's third bridge:
not for vehicular use, but most certainly for walking and cycling.

A man and a boy have found something of interest over the rail – possibly a heron, which can often be seen here.

The Clappers footpath from the weir to Lower Caversham; a rural scene that has hardly changed. The path gives access to View Island nature reserve. There is an interesting old gas lamp standard on the right.

The Clappers footbridge over the millstream; the name is of uncertain origin, but may mean a raised footpath. The timbers of the bridge have been renewed in recent years.

King's Road Bridge along Kennet Side. This photograph was taken in 1974 before the redevelopment of Newtown was started.

Orts Road, Newtown, before redevelopment. The building in the foreground had been the smokehouse of John Eighteen's the fishmonger, but when the photograph was taken, it was being used as a garage. The footpath to the rear of The Fisherman's Cottage pub can be seen on the left.

King's Road with The Lodge Hotel, built in the 1880s as a temperance establishment. It has now been replaced by residential accommodation. The building to the left remains. The Bridgewater Windscreens building has also been converted into apartments.

Back Road, Newtown, which ran between Orts Road and Kennet Side, in 1974. The Victorian dwellings facing onto King's Road had not yet been demolished. Part of Huntley and Palmers can just be seen in the background.

This view of Back Road must have been taken some weeks later.
The True Patriot pub was closed and still standing, but demolition
of houses had already taken place for the redevelopment of Newtown.
In the background are the grand Bath stone houses fronting on
King's Road.

This photograph of Kennet Side can be dated to about 1978, because the housing here was part of Phase 1 of the Newtown redevelopment. Buddleia bushes have already taken root on the guard rail to the river.

The Fisherman's Cottage in 1974. This was one of the four pubs to be retained by the Reading Borough Council's redevelopment brief. It is a Grade II listed building. Just two are still trading today – the Fisherman's and the Jolly Anglers, also on Kennet Side.

The barrier just below Blake's Lock on Kennet Side, taken in 1974. The buildings and gasometer in the background have now been replaced by high-rise residential apartments. The white painted building on the left was the Thames Tavern.

The lock from the now disused gasometer. The spires of St Giles, the Wesley
Methodist Church and St John's (now the Polish Church of the Sacred Heart)
are unchallenged by Blades or other skyscrapers.

This again was taken in about 1974, and shows children reacting to the photographer, somewhere in Newtown.

The last two images in this section feature children playing in Newtown in about 1980, after the redevelopment had taken place. I have included them to show that the area was being used by the children as an informal playground.

Children playing on a guard rail somewhere in Newtown.

St Mary's Butts, Minster Street and some young citizens

Where is the centre of Reading? Two hubs or nodes have claimed the honour at various times: St Mary's Butts, with Reading's oldest church, the Civic Centre and the current open-air market, or the Market Place, boasting the Town Hall, St Laurence's and the site of the Abbey's main gate. This section wanders from one towards the other, west to east. We then double back to the Oxford Road for a complete contrast: scenes in the primary school, full of unselfconscious children.

St Mary's Butts. The street cleaner was a well-known character. The tea kiosk is happily still there, but the three red telephone boxes, designed by Sir Giles Gilbert Scott, have been replaced by two modern ones.

A rainy day in Hosier Street market, with the rear of St Mary's, Castle Street, in the background. The Tourist Information Centre moved to the Town Hall and then St Mary's churchyard before it was abolished.

The same day in the market. What is interesting the traders? At the other end of town, the Market Place now has occasional specialist food markets.

Minster Street from St Mary's churchyard. What is the tubular column
on the right of the pedestrian access used for? It does not seem to be
a lamp standard. Could it be a sewer vent?

Minster Street from Gun Street. The building in the foreground has been demolished and redeveloped as part of the Oracle Shopping Centre. The entrance to the 1628 Oracle workhouse was here, built under the terms of the will of John Kendrick, a Reading cloth merchant, to provide employment for the needy. His legacy also gave rise to the Kendrick Boys' and Girls' Schools in the 1870s.

Minster Street and Yield Hall Lane. The George Hotel, first heard of in the 15th century, has been rebuilt and rearranged under many different owners over the years. The Trades Union building has been demolished; Yield Hall Lane is now pedestrianised.

The entrance to The George. The carriage is no longer in the courtyard. The lamps at the top and on the wall are modern reproductions of gas-lamps.

The next eight photos were all taken in about 1975 at Oxford Road Primary School. The first one shows a girl being very attentive in morning assembly.

Again in assembly, it would seem that the two boys are listening very closely to what is going on.

Whilst the young lad is concentrating on the proceedings, the girl
in the background seems more interested in him!

Assembly is less like a religious service these days, but at some schools pupils still sit on the floor.

A teacher, resplendent with waistcoat and watch-chain, seems to be saying to the young boy 'Where are you going to, young man?' The wall-mounted fire extinguisher is interesting from a modern health and safety point of view!

A candid shot of a girl in a classroom with a teacher in a Fair Isle jumper.
Does anyone still have one of these?

An impromptu lunch-time game of cricket in the playground
with a jumper at the bowler's end and a brick pier for a wicket.

It would seem that the batsman has been given out, as the boy on the extreme right has an index finger raised and the teacher seems to be confirming this.

Queen's Road, Watlington Street, London Street, Crown Street and Southampton Street

Back at the east end of town, we explore Queen's Road and the surrounding streets. As elsewhere, much has come down, much has gone up, and uses have changed, but some old fabric has survived.

Queen's Road from Sidmouth Street in about 1978. The building
to let is the offices of William Kingham Ltd., wholesale grocers.
The Inland Revenue's Sapphire Plaza was still open when this
photograph was taken; HM Revenue and Customs have now closed
all of their enquiry centres. Anyone travelling along Queen's Road
today will see the extent of the rebuilding and redevelopment
which has taken place.

Queen's Road with Trinity Congregational Church and St John's school in the foreground.

Queen's Road roofscapes taken from the roof level of Sapphire Plaza. The small yet interesting building with a pyramidal roof in the centre of the shot is probably part of the old Kendrick Boys' School. The white-painted buildings in the far distance were The Queen's Hotel and the adjacent Dymore Brown's brewery.

This shot shows more of the warehouses and buildings belonging
to William Kingham Ltd., with Kennet House fronting onto the canal.
This building has recently undergone extensive refurbishment, with
completely new facades, for a change of use from offices
into apartments.

Taken from the point where the New Cut, dug in 1802, parts company with the Kennet. Sidmouth Street is in the centre foreground. The entire area at the back became the DHSS offices, which have now been converted to apartments.

Kennet Side from Watlington Street Bridge with King's Point on the right. The buildings on the other side of the canal were the original Inland Revenue offices, demolished to make way for the DHSS redevelopment.

St John's Church, Watlington Street. The Church of England wanted to demolish it when they built the new church of St John the Evangelist and St Stephen in Newtown, but were finally persuaded to sell it to the Polish community.

The church's boundary wall was listed, and the Council refused permission to demolish it; this meant that contractors could not access the site to destroy the church itself.

119–121 London Street in about 1978, when it housed Sargents Embrook, who sold drawing office supplies. Grade II listed, it was the original bakery set up by Joseph Huntley in 1822 before he formed a partnership with George Palmer. It was rebuilt in the very early 1980s, but had to retain the existing architectural features of the original facade.

Inside Sargents Embrook, on the second floor behind the dormer windows. The building was in a very poor state.

Southampton Street and Crown Street with the Red Cow, one of seven Reading pubs listed in Pigot's 1830 Directory that are still trading under the same name. At the time of writing the Red Cow is closed but scheduled to reopen under new management.

Crown Street, with an advertisement for M. Venner & Sons Ltd.,
bacon curers, whose factory was behind the building you can see.
This has since been demolished, together with part of the adjoining
building with an interesting gabled roof and a balcony at first floor
level. The ruined building on the extreme right was originally
the Carpenter's Arms; the flank wall with fireplace can still be seen.

Crown Street, looking towards Pell Street. The Tudor-style building,
then occupied by Guthrie Allsebrook, Water Supply Engineers, was once
St Giles's Parish School, although most of this had been demolished
together with the four-storey office block at the rear.

The junction of London Road and East Street in about 1978. A certain amount of redevelopment of the houses on the right has taken place, but those to the left remain.

A similar view. Many people may remember the Café Ole and the adjoining newsagents; both have gone.

Southampton Street with Hawk Cottages. There were many cramped, unhealthy courts in this area, named for birds, trees and flowers. Hawk Cottages are the last surviving remnant of this early example of arbitrarily themed street-naming.

A miscellany of people, places and puzzles

If you can pinpoint the mystery locations, please contact me via the publisher. The final image, of a girl walking over the Horseshoe Bridge at the confluence of the Thames and Kennet, is included here simply because it is of the lady I met in 1973 in the offices of Broadway & Malyan, and we married in 1976.

Union Street, linking Friar and Broad Streets, is universally known as Smelly Alley. This is the Broad Street end, with Jax of Oxford Street in the background. The Alley, Reading's first pedestrian precinct, remains popular with shoppers.

The Emporium, Merchants Place. Stallholders sold antiques, clothes, ephemera and second-hand books. It is sad to say that while the building is still there, this rather special shop is no longer trading.

A mystery picture.
Does anyone knows where it was?

A view from the offices of Chas. Smith & Son, architects, which were above Drew's, the ironmongers, when they were on the corner of Friar Street and Greyfriars Road. A gentleman with a very interesting barrow is walking along the middle of the road; I hope he survived.

From the same vantage point, two men who are hopefully just talking whilst standing near three planters on the street corner.

Another mystery location.

The gaily-painted 1890s bandstand in the Forbury Gardens.

A smoky pub, a sight not seen since July 2007. But which pub is it?

Messing about on the Thames without lifebelts or jackets.

In King's Road, an advert for a well-known low-alcohol lager.

Three isolated houses in Coley Place. These were built on a steeply sloping site, so are three storeys facing the road but four at the rear. They have escaped redevelopment.

Castle Hill, with Vincent's Garage before it was demolished to make way for Avco House, which is now called Advantage. The roofs of the houses featured in the previous photograph can just be seen over the flat roof of the garage.

Workers on their lunch-time break, presumably engaged in building
the pedestrian bridge over the Inner Distribution Road.

From the IDR bridge, with the brewery maltings in the background, which have been converted to flats. This part of the old Simonds/ Courage brewery site is now mostly residential.

Bright Street, with a malthouse and a horse-drawn dray behind the wall in the background. Such drays were still making local deliveries in the 1960s, and this photograph probably dates from that time.

The Kennet just downstream from Pell Street bridge over the Kennet in the morning sun.

The sun has gone in, the stove is lit … and maybe it's feeding time.

The Forbury Gardens are a lunchtime oasis.

Eldon Square. The park is officially the King George V Memorial Gardens; the statue on the south side, not visible in this shot, is of Lord Reading, Viceroy of India.

The Plasterer's Arms in Rupert Street, a typical Morlands 1930s half-timbered pub. It survived the Newtown redevelopment but was demolished some years later to make way for a rather insignificant block of flats. In the 1960s the licensees were the parents of Melvyn, now Lord Bragg, who helped in the pub at weekends.

Away from the town centre, at the top of Redlands Road, stood Southern Hill, a striking set of six houses pretending to be either one big villa or three smaller ones stuck together. They were probably designed by E W Garbutt, who also did Theale church, in about 1830; here he was clearly influenced by Sir John Soane.

Southern Hill in a very poor state of repair. Most of it belonged to the Council; despite a Grade II listing, demolition was allowed in 1977. Had they survived they would now be very desirable properties in a prime position.

The Horseshoe Bridge, attached to Brunel's railway bridge, was built in 1891 for draught-horses hauling boats up the Thames, taking them across the mouth of the Kennet. This peaceful spot would have been ruined by a 1990s proposal for a major highway known as the Cross Town Route.

Two Rivers Press has been publishing in and about Reading since 1994.
Founded by the artist Peter Hay (1951–2003), the press continues
to delight readers, local and further afield, with its varied list of
individually designed, thought-provoking books.